VIOLET FLAME
TO HEAL
BODY, MIND
& SOUL

VIOLET FLAME
TO HEAL
BODY, MIND
& SOUL

ELIZABETH CLARE PROPHET

SUMMIT UNIVERSITY ⬥ PRESS®

VIOLET FLAME TO HEAL BODY, MIND AND SOUL
by Elizabeth Clare Prophet
Copyright © 1997 by Summit University Press
All rights reserved

Library of Congress Catalog Card Number: 2001099355
ISBN: 0-922729-37-9

SUMMIT UNIVERSITY 🐦 PRESS®

Disclaimer: No guarantee whatsoever is made to anyone by
Summit University Press or Elizabeth Clare Prophet that the
spiritual system of the science of the spoken Word, including
meditation, visualization, dynamic decrees, and spiritual healing,
embodied in this book will yield successful results for anyone at
any time. The functioning of Cosmic Law is a direct experience
between the individual and his own Higher Consciousness. As in
Jesus' time, some were healed and some were not—according to
their faith or lack of it. Karma and the Divine Providence must be
the final arbiter of each one's application of the sacred fire. We
can only witness to our personal healing—body, mind and soul—
through the use of the suggested mantras and spiritual disciplines.
Each man may prove or disprove the Law for himself. The practice and proof of the Science of Being rests with the individual.
No one can do it for another. These spiritual techniques do not
replace medical treatment.

07   06   05   04   03   02   9   8   7   6   5   4

CONTENTS

PREFACE

Once I was on a radio show in Atlanta, where I was interviewed by a clairvoyant. "You have a lot of violet light in your aura," he said. This has happened to me many times since 1961 when I first began using the violet flame. And it wasn't only psychics who noticed the violet. Hindu yogis and Buddhist monks also looked at my late husband, Mark, and me and asked where we had gotten "all of that violet" in our auras.

Of course, the violet light comes from the violet flame, which I learned about from Mark. Since he passed on in 1973, I have shared the secrets of the violet flame with thousands of people all over the world. When you learn these secrets, you too will have violet light in your aura.

The violet flame is more than violet light. It is an invisible spiritual energy that appears violet to those who have developed their spiritual vision. In previous centuries, knowledge of the violet flame was given only to a chosen few who had proven themselves worthy. Saints and adepts of East and West have long used the violet flame to accelerate their spiritual development, but this once-secret knowledge was not revealed to the masses until the twentieth century.

The violet flame has many purposes. It revitalizes and invigorates us. It can heal emotional and even physical problems, improve relationships and make life easier. More important, the violet flame changes negative energy into positive energy, which makes it an effective tool for healing. Today we are learning more than ever before about how disease can be rooted in our mental, emotional and spiritual states. By transforming negative thoughts and feelings, the violet flame provides a platform for our healing.

I call it the highest gift of God to the universe. I think you will agree once you try it for yourself.

Elizabeth Clare Prophet

NOTE: All the stories in this book are real. Some names, however, have been changed at the person's request.

THE VIOLET FLAME HEALS
WOUNDS FROM PAST LIVES

The first time I met Cynthia, she told me
about her past. When she was sixteen she
almost killed her father. The abuse had started when she was little, when she used to sit
on his knee while he combed her curly hair
into ringlets. But then he wanted to do more
than play. And he said he would kill her and
her mother if she ever told anyone. So she
never did.

But she used to wake up screaming, "No,
Daddy!" Her mother never did anything
about it. And Cynthia grew up playing strange
games by herself out under the oak tree by
their white frame home in suburban Illinois.
She buried her Barbie dolls in carefully lined
shoe boxes, marking their graves with pebble
outlines. She would dig them up the next day
and repeat the ritual.

One summer evening Cynthia stayed out

late, walking and holding hands with Rick from geometry class. When she got home and opened the screen door, a painted china dog flew past her and crashed on the faded wood porch. "Where've you been?" Daddy shouted. Before she could make it up the stairs to her room, Daddy slapped her face hard, tore her white blouse and sent a praying-hands bookend sailing past her ear. "Don't ever let me catch you with a boy again! I'll kill him, and I'll kill you too!"

When Cynthia tiptoed down the steps later that night, powder blue suitcase in hand, she could hear Daddy snoring in the living room. She went into the kitchen and slowly opened the glass-knobbed drawer. Daddy always kept the carving knives sharp. She stared at the knives and then at her shadow, the moonlight throwing the image of her bobbed hair large against the wall in front of her. She sighed, quietly closed the drawer, picked up her suitcase and eased herself out the back door.

Cynthia never saw her father again. She went to Chicago, took her GED, waitressed her way through college and was hired at an investment firm. Although she advanced quickly in her career, she knew she hadn't gotten beyond her past.

Cynthia spent one day a month "sick," crying in the closet and thinking about her childhood. A string of relationships ended in failure, and at thirty-five she found herself alone. She was first able to talk about her past to a therapist, looking out of his Wacker Drive office onto Lake Michigan. After a year of therapy in which she told every detail of her past, looking for keys that would help her get beyond the memories, she felt stuck.

Why had all this happened to her? Why did she have an abusive father and a mother who let him abuse her? What did she do to deserve it? Deep down inside, she felt it must be something terrible.

One day as she drifted along the sidewalk lost in thought, someone handed her a violet handbill. "Learn to use the violet flame to transmute painful memories," it said. It was an advertisement for one of my lectures. Cynthia attended and listened to me explain the violet flame and "decrees."

Decrees are rhythmic prayers that call forth a powerful spiritual energy. This light-energy, combined with visualization, has the special quality of erasing and transmuting negative aspects of ourselves.

To *transmute* is to alter in form, appearance or nature, especially to change something into a higher form. The term was used by ancient alchemists who sought to change base metals into gold, separating the "gross" from the "subtle" by means of heat. The most spiritual of the alchemists were in search of a way to change the lead of negative human energy into the gold of divine energy. Some of them accomplished this goal by using the secrets of the violet transmuting flame.

Mystics throughout the ages have known how to use this energy. But it wasn't taught publicly until the 1930s, when Guy and Edna Ballard founded the "I AM" Religious Activity. The Ballards wrote of the violet flame as the "means by which any human being can free himself from his own human discord and imperfection."[1] Mark Prophet, who later founded The Summit Lighthouse, received further revelations on the violet flame that he shared with me when I began working with him in 1961.

During the lecture Cynthia sat toward the back listening to my explanations and reading the decrees carefully. She kept silent as the group repeated them, not sure she wanted to join in.

When Cynthia later decided to use the violet flame for the first time, she was sitting in an olive green armchair in the living room of her Lincoln Park apartment, feet on a stack of *Vogue*s, looking at a framed Georgia O'Keeffe lithograph. She held the booklet in front of her and began to repeat:

> I AM the violet flame
> In action in me now
> I AM the violet flame
> To Light alone I bow
> I AM the violet flame
> In mighty cosmic power
> I AM the light of God
> Shining every hour
> I AM the violet flame
> Blazing like a sun
> I AM God's sacred power
> Freeing every one

"Such a simple rhyme," she thought, "like a nursery rhyme." Cynthia remembered that each time we repeat "I AM the violet flame" (which means "God in me is the violet flame"), we are transforming ourselves so that we can become more closely united with God.

She repeated the decree nine times and then went to bed. The next night at the same time, she tried it again. After a few repetitions she was able to remember the verse without reading it, so she closed her eyes. She sensed a shower of light falling around her. When she finished the decree, she felt tingly all over. After two weeks of giving violet-flame decrees, she felt more at peace with herself. But she was still troubled by flashbacks from her childhood.

Then one night Cynthia had a vivid dream. She saw an image of a black, high-laced boot planting itself in a mud puddle. She felt raindrops pelting her back and watched them make the puddles dance. She walked slowly toward a two-story, Tudor-style house up the road. As the rain soaked through her clothes and trickled down her back, she simply pulled forward her black poke bonnet and walked even more slowly. As she lifted the wooden beam of the gate and went in the back door, Mr. Farnsworth was waiting.

Then she flashed on another scene: Her sobbing and him laughing. Her threatening never to come back. Him threatening to turn her family out of their cottage. Her stabbing him with a kitchen knife as he slept. Her running away to London, later dying in a cold garret.

When she woke up, she could remember the dream, smell the lilacs near the gate and hear the rain splashing in the puddles as she walked toward the house. But she felt lighter and freer, almost as if the rain had washed away the feelings of the past. "Why should I feel so good after such an awful dream?" she asked herself.

It was several months later that Cynthia told me about her childhood and her dream. I explained to her that she had remembered a past life and that it contained karmic seeds of her current life challenges. Mr. Farnsworth had reincarnated as her father. In being born as his daughter, she had balanced, or made up for, the karma she had created by killing him. When she chose not to take the opportunity to kill him again, she had broken the karmic cycle that had tied them together for many lifetimes.

But recalling the karmic record was just the first step in getting beyond her past. She still had spiritual work to do. The memory of the violence, the pain, the grief and the guilt were keeping her from moving on with her life plan. On a spiritual level, the energy that had gone into those emotions had solidified around her soul like black tar.

"Why was I shown this past life now?" asked Cynthia.

"Your soul is ready to deal with the record," I answered. "That's why I recommend using the violet flame rather than hypnotherapy to look into past lives. When you enter a state of hypnotic regression, you may come upon all kinds of memories and thoughts, some not even your own. These could confuse you and lead you off on tangents. When you use the violet flame, you know that God will reveal to you only as much of your past as you are ready to deal with."

"What am I supposed to do with this dream?"

"The dream was shown to you so that you could dissolve the karmic records with the violet flame."

"How do I do that?"

"As you give the violet flame, the scenes from the dream will come up on the screen of your mind. Every time you see those scenes, visualize a giant eraser, like a chalkboard eraser, only violet, rubbing away the picture. After you do this enough times, the memory will stop being painful and gradually fade from the forefront of your mind."

"I'll try it. I'll try anything at this point."

A few weeks later Cynthia called me. She sounded excited. "I had the most amazing experience! It was just after I finished giving my violet-flame decrees. All of these pictures flooded my mind. I could see what happened to me after I died in that London garret. My body felt light, and it floated up into a beam of light. I heard a sound like wind and then

I was in a beautiful place with gardens and flowers. I just stayed there for a while and played with some children."

"Good! You're starting to get beyond the record. Now you need to ask God to reveal to you the next record you should work on so you can get on with your life plan."

"What is my life plan?"

"Your life plan is something that is prepared between one life and the next. Have you heard about the life review that people often go through during near-death experiences?"

"Yes."

"The beings of light who conduct the review are Ascended Masters. These are saints and sages of East and West who once lived on earth, fulfilled their reason for being and ascended, or reunited with God. There are usually eight at the review but the numbers vary, depending on the needs of the soul.

"After the review, they prepare a plan for your next life based on God's original plan for you and what you did (positive or negative) in your preceding lives. They tell you that you will be put into a situation where you will have to meet karmic challenges. If you overcome them, you will go on to the next level of challenges in your spiritual evolution. If you stumble—for instance, if you had killed your father or even killed yourself out of guilt feelings—you will have to come back to face the same obstacle again."

Cynthia and I had several more conversations. She began to feel better about her past. She was able to visit her mother, talk to her about the abuse and forgive her for not intervening. She no longer gets debilitated by flashbacks, and she is more positive about the future. Although her story isn't neatly wrapped up in a wedding dress, she has developed a relationship with a strong and caring man.

THE SECRET OF THE VIOLET FLAME

Cynthia is one of thousands of people who have transformed their lives with the violet flame. You can recognize them the instant you meet them—young and old, from five- and six-year-olds who have just begun repeating the shortest violet-flame mantras to those who have been giving violet-flame decrees for forty years. There is an extra spring to their step, an extra sparkle in their eyes. They have a secret.

Bill learned this secret from books published by the "I AM" Religious Activity. He was on Maui in 1971 investigating a variety of spiritual paths when someone handed him a copy of Guy Ballard's *Unveiled Mysteries*, written under the pen name Godfré Ray King. Bill began reading the book and was amazed to find that he could actually see violet light coming out of the pages. "This was like a spiritual sign to me that I was on the right track," he recalls. Through The Summit Lighthouse, Bill later learned more about the violet flame and has been invoking it ever since.

Other people have also had a sensory confirmation of the presence of the violet flame. Steve saw a huge column of violet light appear around me after one of my lectures. Gardy, a computer programmer, saw violet light emanating from his keyboard the first time he invoked the violet flame. Adrian heard a sound like a waterfall.

Not everyone who gives the violet flame sees violet light or hears unusual sounds. Some sense violet when they close their eyes and focus on the energy center between their eyebrows. Others simply feel happier or more in tune with their Higher Self.

The violet flame imparts a feeling of élan —of vibrancy, buoyancy and vitality. It helps you to be merciful and forgiving. How does it do this? By transmuting your negative karma.

Negative energy can manifest as everything from disease or accidents to ingrained habit patterns that keep you from getting along with others. This negativity is recorded in your aura, which is the energy field that surrounds your physical body. The aura reflects positive thoughts and feelings, but it can also reflect feelings such as anger, hatred, jealousy or frustration. This includes vibrations you pick up from those around you as well as your own accumulated karma and records of past lives.

So you could be walking around all day with the anger sent to you by a grumpy cabdriver or with your own frustration over an argument that you and your spouse had during breakfast. Or, as we saw in Cynthia's story, you may be unhappy because you're carrying the burden of traumatic experiences, either from this life or past lives. This negative energy solidifies and collects around you. It can weigh you down, like a pair of cement overshoes.

But it doesn't just cover your feet. This negativity resembles a kettledrum-shaped vortex of energy that surrounds you from your waist down. I call it the electronic belt. Psychologists call it the subconscious and the unconscious. As in the case of Cynthia, this accumulated negative energy may keep you from being successful in this life.

The solution is the violet flame, the "miracle solvent" that dissolves negative energy. Giving five to fifteen minutes of violet-flame decrees in the morning or evening will help you maintain a feeling of peace throughout the day no matter what happens to you.

Once you have begun to use the violet flame to clean up your aura, you will discover that it can create positive change at all levels of your being. The violet flame can free you to progress spiritually, to enjoy the full benefit of positive energy descending from your God Presence and to realize your highest potential. Uniting with your Higher Self can take many years or even lifetimes. But each time you invoke the violet flame, you are bringing yourself closer to that goal.

The more you give violet-flame decrees, the more you free yourself from limiting conditions. Then you, as an instrument of God's love, are better able to help others. You will find that when people contact your aura, they too will receive healing and upliftment.

The true purpose of miracles is to restore wholeness to the body and to achieve union with the Higher Self. Jesus used the power of the Holy Spirit to work his miracles. The first miracle he performed was at the marriage feast in Cana of Galilee, where he turned water into wine.

The water symbolized the human consciousness being transformed into the violet wine of the Holy Spirit. This is a clue that Jesus was using the violet-flame aspect of the Holy Spirit to perform this miracle. Once you are transformed by the violet flame, you, the alchemist, can also perform miracles of spiritual and physical healing.

*The violet flame goes after
the schisms which cause psycho-
logical problems that go back to
early childhood and previous
incarnations and that have estab-
lished such deep grooves within
the consciousness that in fact
they have been difficult to shake
lifetime after lifetime.*

—Saint Germain

THE EYES OF CHILDREN

*B*arbara first began giving violet-flame decrees out of a sense of desperation. Ever since she was a teenager, she felt depressed during the month of January, and each year seemed worse than the last. "In January I just wanted to crawl under my bed and not come out," she says. Barbara's sister, who had been giving the violet flame for eighteen years, assured her that it would help cure her January funks.

One October, Barbara sat down with a tape of decrees, *Save the World with Violet Flame 1*, and a booklet with the words to the decrees. She started the tape and began giving the violet flame. Barbara didn't think that she was accomplishing much since she was getting tongue-tied and couldn't keep up with the tape. Suddenly she had a startling confirmation that something was happening.

She was in her office at home and the rest

of the family was in the basement. Her children didn't know that she was giving decrees. They didn't know what decrees were. Her eight-year-old son, Nathan, came to the top of the basement stairs and started calling her. She turned off the tape and came out to see what he needed. He stared at her. "Mom! Your hair—it's purple!" She looked at her hair. It still looked blonde to her.

"Really?" she said. "Yes!" he answered. Later she asked him if he really saw purple. "I saw purple all around you, Mom," he said.

As she continued giving decrees during the next few days, Nathan told her that everyone in the house and all of the rooms looked purple. She decided that he must be one of those children who are able to see into the spiritual world and she shared the secret of decrees with him. He asked her to do them in his room while he was going to sleep. He soon memorized some decrees and began giving them himself.

Not only did the violet flame transform

her home, it also transformed her state of mind during the following January. Even though she was unemployed and low on money, she was happy. "I could have felt so depressed," she recalls, "but the violet flame helped me psychologically and helped us to keep the harmony in our home." By March she had found a job that she loved, and two years later she is still giving her violet-flame decrees.

SPIRITUAL PROTECTION
FROM THE VIOLET FLAME

$\mathcal{K}$athleen had firsthand experience with the violet flame's protective power. She had been giving decrees for a few years when she was invited to a company party with entertainment provided by a psychic. She decided that she did not want him to be able to see into her aura and read her thoughts and feelings; she liked her privacy. Before going to the party, she gave a decree for protection and visualized the violet flame filling her aura.

The psychic began giving uncannily accurate readings of the guests at the party. "He spoke to each person individually, correctly naming and identifying various family members, sometimes telling factual stories about a recent incident in someone's life," Kathleen recalls. However, when the psychic got to her, he made a vague comment and skipped to the next person.

Why didn't the psychic read her aura? Her boss told her the next day: "The psychic said that it was easy to read the other people's minds. Their thoughts were dangling in their auras, hanging around the outer edges. But not yours. When he looked at your aura, all he could see was a violet light."

SAINT GERMAIN'S GIFT
OF THE VIOLET FLAME

The Ascended Masters, together with the angels and Archangels, teach us how to liberate ourselves and others. From spiritual worlds, these Masters have communicated to us through various Messengers. Both Mark and I were trained to receive messages from the Masters, which we call dictations.

The Masters have also dictated many of the decrees that we use. When you recite their actual words, you have direct access to their protection, guidance and blessing.

Each Ascended Master teaches us about a different aspect of God. Saint Germain, who has been the inspiring force—if not the key player—in freedom movements throughout the millennia, has shown us how to use the violet flame to free ourselves and all mankind.

The violet flame is the essence of one of

SAINT GERMAIN

the "seven rays." Just as a ray of sunlight passing through a prism is refracted into the seven colors of the rainbow, so spiritual light manifests as seven rays. Each ray has a specific color, frequency and quality of God's consciousness. The violet ray is known as the seventh ray. When you invoke it in the name of God, it descends as a beam of spiritual energy and bursts into a spiritual flame in your heart as the qualities of mercy, forgiveness, justice, freedom and transmutation.

Saint Germain is known as the Lord of the Seventh Ray. Each time we pray to him, he brings us many gifts of the Spirit—his joy, diplomacy and creativity. He can inspire us with his innovations in science, literature, religion, government, philosophy, education, healing, alchemy and other fields.

For almost seventy years, Saint Germain has been preparing us to enter into the age of Aquarius, an era of peace, freedom and enlightenment. He appeared to Guy Ballard in the early 1930s and gave him the first teaching on the violet flame.

Saint Germain said that after centuries of keeping the knowledge of the violet flame secret, the Masters had decided to release its use to the public during this crucial time. Saint Germain has said, "The use of the violet consuming flame is more valuable to you and to all mankind than all the wealth, all the gold and all the jewels of this planet."[2]

EXPERIENCING
THE VIOLET FLAME

*A*t study centers around the world, people gather every week to give decrees for the violet flame. Invoking the violet flame in a group multiplies the power of the decrees, and people say they feel a more powerful energy. Anyone is welcome to join these sessions and experiment further with the power of this miracle solvent.

Spiritual seekers also enjoy attending my lectures about the teachings of the Ascended Masters and the use of decrees, which I conduct periodically around the country.

Jeff had a life-changing experience at one such lecture. He had never seen me speak before and was not prepared for the powerful violet-flame energy he felt as I began giving a transfer of light from Saint Germain to those present.

As Jeff joined the line of people waiting

to pass in front of me, he felt a surge of light. At the same moment, his friend Steve gasped. He had seen, with his spiritual sight, a huge column of violet flame descend from above and surround both me and the altar behind me. Although Jeff couldn't see it, he could feel it. His cells tingled in response to the violet flame.

When he got about fifteen feet away from the altar, he recalls, "I was immersed by this shower of violet flame. My body became cleansed and more alive than I had ever felt before." For Jeff, the tangible presence of the violet flame was a memory that would stay with him for a long time.

HOW DOES
THE VIOLET FLAME WORK?

*B*en and Carol own a shop in a busy mall. They and their family regularly give violet-flame decrees, and they say that it helps to bring customers into their store and makes the customers feel happier when they leave.

"Sometimes nobody will be coming into the shop," says Carol. "People will walk right by and they don't even seem to see us. Then we go in the back and say our prayers. We come out and it's almost miraculous. The place will be filled with people."

The people seem to get an energy boost just by coming into the shop when it's filled with violet-flame energy. "People who look so burdened that you couldn't get a smile out of them, no matter what, are smiling; and we feel the same way," says Carol.

After she gives violet-flame decrees, Carol says that she notices a change in the atmosphere. "Something of a transcendent nature takes place. I'm sure that eventually science will discover what it is that happens when we invoke the violet flame."

People do notice a spiritual and physical difference when they use the violet flame. But what actually happens when we repeat the words of a violet-flame decree?

I can give you two perspectives on this—the spiritual perspective as it has been revealed to me by the Ascended Masters and a scientific perspective based on recent developments in physics and medicine. Both explanations involve the concept of vibration.

In physics, vibration is the speed at which something moves back and forth, or oscillates. As I understand it, at a spiritual level vibration is also the rate of spin of the electrons as they move around the nucleus of the atom. As we will see, these definitions may not be far apart.

We each have four bodies that are envelopes of our soul: (1) the physical body, which we can see and touch; (2) the desire, or astral, body, which contains our emotions; (3) the mental body, which is our conscious mind; and (4) the etheric, or memory, body, which contains the memories of all of our past lives. The violet flame works on these four lower bodies by changing the rate of their vibration.

Saint Germain has given us the violet-flame decree "I AM a being of violet fire! I AM the purity God desires!" When you recite this and other violet-flame decrees, the violet flame permeates every cell and atom of your body, into your mind, your emotions, your subconscious and your memory.

What does the violet flame do when it permeates your atoms? The Masters have given the following explanation.

We all know that atoms are mostly empty space. If an atom were the size of a basketball, its nucleus would still be too small for our eyes to see. Yet 99.9 percent of the mass of the atom is concentrated in the

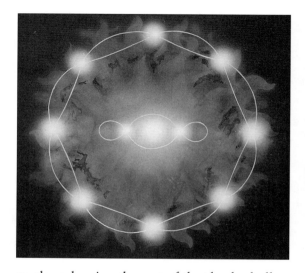

nucleus, leaving the rest of that basketball as empty space, inhabited solely by electrons, which weigh very little. All that empty space between the nucleus and the edge of the atom is where discord and negative energy can become stuck.

At the cellular and molecular level, this substance appears as dust, soot, tar or even cement. The Masters have used the illustration of someone taking a pail of molten tar and pouring it over a barrel full of marbles. The space between the marbles gets gummed up by the tar running down, and soon the whole mass is welded together.

The Masters tell us that when our physical and spiritual bodies become clogged by negative energy and karma, it slows down the vibration of the electrons in our four lower bodies. We then begin to resonate more with negativity and less with the pure cosmic energy that comes from our God Presence, and eventually we can become ill. The more substance there is in our four lower bodies, the lower our rate of vibration and the more burdened we become. Spiritually, this is why people die.

If you have studied acupuncture and yoga, you know that optimum health comes when spiritual energy is flowing freely through our bodies. When karmic substance solidifies, it's like the hardening of the arteries of our spiritual bodies. When we resonate with this negativity, we will gradually become it unless we do something to turn ourselves around.

The violet fire transmutes anything negative that is lodged anywhere in your spiritual or physical being. This includes everything from kernels of self-hatred to physical viruses. When the violet flame goes to work, it passes through the clogged spaces between the electrons and the nuclei. It ejects these particles of dense substance from your body and dissolves them. This process transmutes the negative energy into positive energy and restores it to its native purity.

THE VIOLET FLAME ACTS LIKE
A POWERFUL DETERGENT

$\mathcal{T}$he violet flame works a little like soap. Soap gets dirt out of your clothes by using the positive and negative charges of atoms. It works because each of its molecules has two sides—a side that is attracted to dirt and a side that is attracted to water. The dirt-loving side attracts the dirt, like a magnet attracts paper clips when it is dragged through a box of them. The water-loving side sticks to the water, carrying the dirt with it.

When we invoke the violet flame, it sets up a polarity between the nucleus of the atom and the white-fire core of the flame. The nucleus, being matter, assumes the negative pole; the white-fire core of the violet flame, being Spirit, assumes the positive pole.

The interaction between the nucleus of the atom and the light in the violet flame establishes an oscillation. This oscillation dislodges the densities that are trapped between the electrons orbiting the nucleus. As this hardened substance that weighs down the atom is loosened, it is thrown into the violet flame and carried away.

But unlike soap, the violet flame does not simply surround and remove the debris; it transforms it into pure light-energy. Freed of this debris, the electrons begin to move more freely, thus raising our vibration and propelling us into a more spiritual state of being.

In one moment you sit surrounded with every kind of negative thought in your aura. In the next, you decide to invoke the violet flame.

And lo! the mighty power of the seventh ray, as a giant electrode of cosmic energy, begins to form around your person. The violet-flame angels gather around you. With palms outstretched, they direct across your four lower bodies and your aura an arc of the violet ray. As that arc flashes across your being, it vaporizes the negative conditions. They literally disappear from heart and mind!

—Archangel Zadkiel

PHYSICAL HEALING WITH THE VIOLET FLAME

*T*oday we are used to the idea that energy rays and forcefields can be used to change and affect matter. In the realm of science fiction, there is *Star Trek* with its tractor and transporter beams and *Batman* with Mr. Freeze's cryonic energy beam that turns people into ice.

While these may seem far-fetched and impossible to us, we can do things today with energy that would have seemed equally far-fetched to most people in the last century—things like transmitting sound through the air via radio waves, heating food with microwaves or taking pictures of bones with X rays.

We know that energy frequencies on the electromagnetic spectrum have beneficial uses. Ultraviolet light, while harmful to our unprotected skin, can be used for healing. Wounds that are treated with ultraviolet light heal faster than those treated with regular medical care alone.

Ultraviolet-light treatments have also been shown to relieve intense skin itching known as pruritus. And ultraviolet light has been used to disinfect the air in hospitals to prevent transmission of tuberculosis and other dangerous diseases. It kills the tuberculosis bacteria in the air.

The action of the violet flame cannot be measured scientifically. But it may work in a similar way to the various frequencies of electromagnetic energy. When a wave passes through a pond, it causes ripples. When microwave energy passes through food, it speeds up the electrons in the food, which causes the food to heat up.

When the violet flame passes through our bodies, it too causes change. By removing calcified emotional debris and other substance, it may allow our bodies to reconnect with their natural healing mechanism. Keep that in mind as you read the following story.

Grace had been struggling with asthma for thirty years. She had been improving her diet and giving the violet flame daily for some time, but she felt that something was blocking her healing. Every night a tightness filled her lungs and she had to reach for her inhaler and sometimes a pulmo-aide and stronger medicine.

One day Grace realized that perhaps her resentment of a former boyfriend was connected to her asthma. He had ignored her even though she had made herself over, hoping to please him. So she resented him and felt sorry for herself.

After she saw the connection between her negative emotions and her physical condition, she gave about ninety minutes of violet-flame decrees and asked to be forgiven for tying up so much energy in this failed relationship. She visualized herself putting this grudge and her self-pity into a giant violet-flame bonfire. She felt all her emotional knots being dissolved and consumed.

The physical effects were dramatic. As she recalls, "About two days later, I was thinking it was time to get a refill for my inhaler. That's when I realized that I hadn't even used it in two days."

Grace hasn't had an asthma attack since. "What's more," she says, "I've been exposed to house dust, fall pollens and chemicals. I've choked on food, laughed with abandon and even gone for walks—all with no problem. In short, I am like a normal person, free to breathe the breath of life again."

The improvement in Grace's life did not come until she identified and resolved the unhappiness that was holding her back. And it was her systematic use of the violet flame that paved the way for her miraculous healing. How does the violet flame do this? It may help us to access a vibrational state in which our body can heal itself.

THE VIOLET FLAME—HELPING OUR BODIES TO HEAL THEMSELVES

*W*e aren't surprised when our body begins manufacturing new skin to heal a cut or when it starts creating new bone to heal a fracture. But we are surprised when something like cancer disappears from our body for no apparent reason. Doctors call this spontaneous remission.

Some doctors who have studied such cases have concluded that it happens when the body is able to access a state in which the cells can use their natural ability for self-repair. They speculate that these healings happen when mind, or consciousness, directs the body to heal itself—the so-called mind/body connection.

What is "mind"? Candace Pert, a molecular biologist who studies the process by which we begin to feel emotions, calls the mind "some kind of enlivening energy in the information realm throughout the brain and body that enables the cells to talk to each other, and the outside to talk to the whole organism."[3]

Pert believes that the mind is located throughout the brain and body, not just above the neck. She sees the emotions as the connection between the mind and the body.

Scientists have demonstrated that the immune system has an intelligence of its own. They don't know why some people's immune systems choose to fight disease while other people's give in to it.

Andrew Weil, a Harvard-trained doctor who studies the mind/body connection, says he believes that if spontaneous healing can happen to one person, it can happen to all. "All the circuitry and machinery is there. The challenge is to discover how to turn on the right switches to activate the process," he says.[4] If we can figure out how to influence this "mind," we can turn on our body's natural healing mechanism.

I believe that disease occurs when the body is vibrating at a different rate from this mind and thus is unable to communicate with the Higher Self. The explanation for healings like Grace's may simply be that the violet flame restores the natural resonance between the Higher Self and the physical body.

HIGHER-DIMENSIONAL PHYSICS
SHEDS LIGHT ON THE MIRACLE
OF THE VIOLET FLAME

*M*ost scientists aren't ready to buy into the idea that energy vibrations can change our health. But recently a scientific theory, the theory of superstrings, has emerged which says that our physical bodies, which seem so solid to us, are nothing more than a collection of vibrations of strings that exist in several dimensions. If this is so, then we can easily understand how the violet flame could heal us by changing our vibrations.

Much of modern physics has been devoted to discovering the true nature of matter and energy. Every time physicists think they have found the smallest particle of matter, a smaller one appears.

In the last century scientists thought that atoms were the smallest particles. Then they discovered that atoms consisted of electrons circling around a nucleus. Next they learned how to split apart the protons and neutrons at the nucleus of the atom, and nuclear energy was released. But scientists have discovered at least sixty more subatomic particles—such as neutrinos, leptons, bosons and quarks—so many that they are sometimes termed a particle zoo.

If superstring theory is correct, we may never find the smallest particle. This theory, which has been evolving since the late sixties, tells us that what seem like particles to us may actually be the vibrating modes of strings—strings that we cannot see, even under a microscope, because they are so tiny. Each string is 100 billion billion times smaller than a proton, so the strings look like particles to us.

Just as the strings of a musical instrument can vibrate at different frequencies and create notes and their harmonics, so these superstrings can vibrate at different frequencies, each one corresponding to a different kind of subatomic particle.

Thus, superstring theory is an elegant way to explain the existence of so many kinds of subatomic particles. They are not different kinds of matter at all. For they are, as physicist Michio Kaku writes, "nothing but the harmonies created by this vibrating string."[5] Scientists like Kaku say that we can only see the particle and not the whole string because the rest of the string is curled up into higher-dimensional space.

Scientists are looking for ways to test superstring theory, which raises as many questions as it answers. But the idea that we are the product of vibrating strings may help explain why people have such remarkable results when they raise their vibration by using the violet flame.

Someday scientists may be able to measure the subtle concentrations of energy that make up our four lower bodies. Or they may be able to measure the energy that descends when we repeat the words of a violet-flame decree. Until then, we can experiment with the violet flame as a powerful form of spiritual energy. It enables us to reestablish our harmony and equilibrium so that we can rediscover what spiritual and physical wholeness really is.

Through these scientific explanations, you have begun to glimpse how the violet flame works. And if you haven't decided to try it yet, read the next story.

A Skeptic Experiments with the Violet Flame

When science and religion seemed to conflict, Darryl dropped religion. He had joined a fundamentalist Christian church in his teens but couldn't reconcile its teachings on creationism with what he was learning about evolution. He also couldn't accept that those who don't follow the Christian message are doomed to hell. "It was a very narrow viewpoint of life," he recalls.

After giving up on religion, however, he became cynical about life and cared only about living for the moment. Although he finished college and began grad school, he dropped out soon after, feeling that he wanted more of a social life. After he got a job as a research associate in the college's agriculture department, he began a life of aimless partying.

Several years later he discovered the teachings of the Ascended Masters and the violet flame. This helped him reclaim his spirituality and his motivation without threatening his scientific beliefs.

He was attracted to Eastern spirituality and particularly to Masters outside the Western tradition. He attended a lecture on the teachings of the Ascended Masters but was reluctant to try decrees.

Then he went to a dictation in which I delivered a message from Serapis Bey, an Egyptian Master. Serapis challenged those present to experiment with the violet flame for six months. "You won't remember in six months where you were when you started, you will be so many miles from the point of your origin," he said.

Darryl was intrigued, so he began giving fifteen minutes of violet-flame decrees every day. Before long, he did notice a difference. He quit drinking, became more motivated and creative at work, and felt his life being filled with a new sense of joy and purpose. He also reformulated his goals to become less materialistic and more spiritual.

"I remember looking back after six months and being amazed by how much I had changed," he says. "I figure that if I had kept on the way I had been going, I'd be an alcoholic, or nearly so, or have AIDS. So I feel that the violet flame has definitely put my life in the right direction."

Darryl has resumed his graduate studies and has also regained an appreciation of Christianity. He realizes that it is not Jesus' teachings that he objects to, only the narrow fundamentalist interpretation of Christianity.

The Difference between Decrees and Eastern Mantras

For thousands of years mystics have believed that repeating sacred words and prayers would propel them into union with God. They also used mantras for ailments of mind and body. Hindu and Buddhist monks repeated mantras for healing everything from depression to fevers.

People who have tried both decrees and Eastern mantras say that decrees have a much more immediate and tangible effect. Martha used Eastern meditation and mantras for twenty-three years. She repeated the Hindu Gayatri mantra, one of the most sacred verses of the Rig-Veda, nearly six thousand times a day. Several years ago she began using the violet flame. Now she repeats the violet-flame mantra "I AM a being of violet fire! I AM the purity God desires!" as many times a day as she can.

"Chanting and decreeing are two different things," she says. She believes both are necessary but now devotes the bulk of her time to decreeing. Chanting gives her a feeling of devotion. But she believes that decrees accomplish more, no matter what the goal—especially the fundamental goal of the mystics, union with God. Decrees help to remove obstacles on the spiritual path, such as fear, pride, selfishness and lack of self-esteem. "Decreeing," she says, "is what really gets it done."

Margaret left her position as a college dean to enter a Zen Buddhist monastery because of stress in her job and in her personal life. Although she felt healed by the routine of chanting and meditation, she concluded that it was an escape. "I knew that I needed to take a more active role in changing myself and the world," she says.

After she left the monastery, she discovered decrees and began using them. She has continued with them for ten years, learning how to direct the energy of her decrees to heal others as well as planet earth. "When you decree, it allows God to work through you," she says.

HOW CHRONIC BACK PAIN WAS HEALED BY SAINT GERMAIN AND THE VIOLET FLAME

*M*ariko's challenges began when she was in her early teens, with the beginning of World War II. Although she was born in America, her parents were Japanese. After Japan bombed Pearl Harbor in December 1941, the Japanese Americans living on the West Coast were placed in internment camps. Mariko and her family were held in one of these camps for three and a half years. Instead of succumbing to boredom, she busied herself teaching classical Japanese dance to the other inmates.

After the war she became a successful businesswoman, but she felt that something was lacking. She began a quest, looking for a spiritual teacher. She thought that this person might be at a university, so she enrolled in college. After receiving a bachelor's degree and a master's degree in education, she began teaching public school.

While Mariko was teaching, she was challenged again. She severely injured her back while putting together a bulletin board in the classroom where she taught gifted junior high school students.

She had been standing on a chair on top of a table and was getting down. As she stood on the table and lowered the chair to the floor, it slipped from her grasp and landed with its legs up. Then she lost her balance and began to fall on top of it. She twisted to protect her heart and ended up landing on her back.

Although she was in great pain, she insisted on going back to work right away so she wouldn't miss the first week of school. This experience seemed to her like the return of a severe karma, but she didn't know the cause.

Mariko had been raised a Buddhist; however, her mother had also taught her to respect Christianity. She believes that God and the Buddhist deity of mercy, Kannon, or Kuan Yin, helped her to get through those first few weeks of school.

That year was a success. The school received the School of Excellence Award from the president of the United States. But Mariko's back injury continued to bother her from time to time, so she knew that the karma behind it was unresolved.

Her spiritual search led her to The Summit Lighthouse. She began giving violet-flame decrees every day but soon had a recurrence of the injury. She wrenched her back while moving a heavy table, but the pain was not as excruciating as before. Mariko continued to decree for the transmutation of the karma and she felt that the violet-flame angels, along with Kuan Yin and Mother Mary, were helping her.

Little by little the true cause of her pain was revealed to her. She realized that she had carried on her back the burdens of others that were not hers to bear. By doing this, she had interfered with their ability to overcome their own problems and thus grow spiritually.

"Then one day I was shown," she says, "like slides slowly moving in front of my eyes (yet I think I was half asleep), what seemed like an entire picture of my karmic debt, which was pertinent to my...back injuries. Perhaps it was from several lifetimes as well as my present life."

Soon after, she experienced a dictation by Saint Germain and felt a healing miracle take place. "I could feel Saint Germain's violet-flame angels repairing and renewing the rent in my back. First vertically and then horizontally, like patchwork, the healing process went on, very slowly, until the rent in my back was totally mended and healing had taken place. I felt no pain while this miraculous healing process was being performed. In fact, I was in heavenly bliss!"

After this experience Mariko was able to

sleep soundly without pain. It has now been two years since the healing and she believes that her problem has been healed for good, thanks to Saint Germain and the violet flame.

As you begin to use the violet flame, you will experience feelings of joy, lightness, hope and newness of life, as though clouds of depression were being dissolved by the very sun of your own being....

The violet flame forgives as it frees, consumes as it transmutes, clears the records of past karma (thus balancing your debts to life), equalizes the flow of energy between yourself and other lifestreams, and propels you into the arms of the living God.

—El Morya

NINE STEPS FOR PUTTING THE VIOLET FLAME INTO ACTION IN YOUR LIFE

1. Set aside a time each day to give violet flame.

You can give violet-flame decrees anywhere, anytime—in your car, while doing chores or before going to bed. In fact, simply repeating a violet-flame mantra anytime you feel tense, tired or irritated can make the difference. But you will get the greatest benefit from the violet flame if you set aside at least fifteen minutes a day to decree without interruption.

It's best to decree in a place dedicated to spiritual work, such as a chapel or a well-lit, clean and aired room. Poor lighting, dust, untidiness and stale air impede the flow of spiritual energy.

On your altar you can put candles, crystals, flowers and photographs of saints, Ascended Masters and your loved ones.

2. Begin your violet-flame session with a prayer.

Before you begin your decrees, give a prayer, or invocation, asking the Ascended Masters, angels and elementals to come and help you.

The elementals are the nature spirits of fire, air, water and earth who are responsible for taking care of our planet. Elementals who represent the fire element are called salamanders; those who represent the air element, sylphs; those who represent the water element, undines; those who represent the earth element, gnomes. They are only too happy to help us clean up both our auras and the planet with the violet flame.

3. Invoke protection before you start using the violet flame.

Remember Barbara? She began giving violet-flame decrees and soon her son saw everyone in the house turn purple. Not too long after she began giving them, her son told her that he could see clouds of darkness attempting to enter the house.

Barbara phoned her sister, who had been giving decrees for a number of years, and learned an important lesson: Never invoke the violet flame without first calling for protection. The Masters teach that when you bring forth more light, darkness is drawn to it, as if by a magnet.

So you need to seal your aura with the white and blue protective energy. One of the best ways to do this is to invoke the tube of light and the protection of Archangel Michael.

Give your tube of light decree each morning and repeat it as necessary throughout the day. As you give it, visualize the dazzling white light from your I AM Presence, the Presence of God above you, forming an impenetrable wall of light around you.

Your prayer to Archangel Michael can be as simple as "Archangel Michael, Help me! help me! help me!" As the Archangel of the first ray, Archangel Michael embodies the qualities of faith, protection, perfection and the will of God. Archangel Michael has personally saved my life a dozen times that I know of and probably thousands of times that I am not aware of.

So give your decrees with joy and gusto and know that when you call to Archangel Michael and his legions of angels, they will immediately be at your side. (See pages 89–90 for the "Tube of Light" decree and decrees to Archangel Michael.)

4. Begin your violet-flame decree with a preamble.

The preamble to a decree is like an invitation. In it we lovingly ask the violet-flame beings— Ascended Masters and angels—for help and guidance.

We generally begin our decrees by saying, "In the name of the beloved mighty victorious Presence of God, I AM in me, and my very own beloved Holy Christ Self..." and include our favorite Masters and saints. Our connection to them is through our I AM Presence and Holy Christ Self.

The I AM Presence is our permanent, perfect God Presence. The Holy Christ Self is our Higher Self and inner teacher who initiates and guides our soul on her path to union with God.

Here is a preamble that you can use and add to:

In the name of the beloved mighty victorious Presence of God, I AM in me, and my very own beloved Holy Christ Self, I call to beloved Saint Germain and the angels of the seventh ray. I ask you to_____.

I ask that my call be multiplied and used to assist all souls on this planet who are in need.

I thank you and I accept it done this hour in full power, according to the will of God.

5. Give the decree slowly at first, then speed up as you give more repetitions of the decree.

The first time you give a decree, you will want to repeat it slowly and deliberately. Endow each word with intense love for God. There is great power in giving a decree slowly. But there is a different power that comes as you gradually increase the speed and raise the pitch of the decree.

Mark Prophet used to compare this acceleration to a train. It starts out "chug... chug" and pretty soon it's going "chug-a-chug-a" and then "chug-chug-chug-chug!" The faster it goes, the greater the action.

As you increase the speed of your decrees, you will find that they are more effective in raising your vibration. The increase in speed should not be artificial. It should feel natural to you; the decree should almost speed itself up.

If you try any of the *Save the World with Violet Flame* tapes listed in the back of this book, you will hear the correct way to increase your speed.

6. Use visualizations to assist your spiritual work.

Most people don't see the violet flame in action with their physical eyes. But when you close your eyes and concentrate on the energy center between your eyebrows, you can sometimes "see" the violet flame at work with your inner eye.

To people who have developed their spiritual sight, the violet flame looks like fire, in colors ranging from dark indigo and brilliant amethyst to violet pink. You may see these flames burning through karmic debris.

Sometimes it helps to imagine this debris as chunks of wood or chunks of tarry substance breaking off from your electronic belt and crackling in the flame. They tumble and bounce and then disappear in a puff of white smoke.

Once you have memorized some of the violet-flame decrees, you can close your eyes and try the following visualizations.

Visualizations:

A Violet-Flame Pillar

When you invoke the violet flame, you can visualize yourself surrounded by a violet-flame pillar about six feet in diameter and about nine feet high. It can extend from beneath your feet to well over the top of your head.

See the violet flame come to life as if you were looking at a movie. The flames rise and pulsate around you in different shades of purple, pink and violet.

Around this violet-flame pillar, you can see your tube of light, an even bigger pillar of white light that protects and seals the violet flame.

Keep this visualization in mind while you

are decreeing and throughout the day. Every time you think of it, you are reinforcing this image.

Healing by the Whirling Violet-Flame Spheres

This visualization can help heal your four lower bodies. As you give a violet-flame decree, imagine a large sphere of violet light forming around you. As you speed up the decree, see the sphere begin to whirl like a tilt-a-whirl at an amusement park. See it spinning faster and faster. This visualization steps up the violet flame and accelerates the vibration of your cells, atoms and electrons.

Next see smaller violet-flame spheres superimposed over each organ in your body. See the action of the violet-flame spheres removing any darkness that may be the basis of disease and consuming it instantly. Then see the violet flame perfecting your organs.

Ask your I AM Presence and Holy Christ Self and the violet-flame angels to sustain

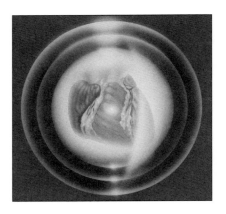

these violet-flame spheres around you throughout the day. Reinforce your request with periodic revisualization of the spheres. Experiment with this visualization and see how it makes you feel.

7. Use violet flame every day.

One of the best times to give your decrees is in the early morning. You'll find that if you decree first thing in the morning, your day will go much smoother.

You can make a specific request for the

transmutation of whatever mental, emotional or physical problems you are working on in your life. You can work on relationships with your friends and loved ones.

8. Use the violet flame to heal the records of past lives.

After you have been giving the violet flame for some time, you may find yourself recalling past lives. Recalling a past life is not something to be taken lightly. When you become aware of it, the karma (positive and negative) of that life comes to the surface.

The negative karma is like Pandora's box. Once you open it, you will want to roll up your sleeves, spend your time serving life and make calls to the violet-flame angels each day to transmute the karmic debris. It can take as little as six months of concentrated violet-flame decrees to balance the karma of one past life. This is indeed a great gift that is given to us by Saint Germain.

As you give the violet flame, pictures of

past lives may come before your mind. You may see yourself as you were in ages long past. Or you may just have the impression that you were in a particular time or place. If the records are painful—and they usually are because your soul is crying out for resolution —you may feel sadness or regret. But you will also feel liberated because you know that as you give your violet-flame decrees, you are transmuting the records of your past karma.

When you become aware of these memories, do not attempt to suppress them. Instead, focus your attention on the light in your heart. Imagine the memory being saturated with the violet flame until the form disappears. Then let go of the memory and let a bright white sun replace it in your mind's eye. You may also want to use the eraser visualization that I gave to Cynthia (see page 14).

There are two elements you are transmuting when you use the violet flame to deal with past karmic records. The first is the emotional and soul memory of the events that are causing you pain. The second is the karmic energy that binds you to those you have hurt or to those who have hurt you. I like to call this the "cause, effect, record and memory" of karma, which includes all energy that you have tied up in negative thoughts or feelings about the past.

Past-life records are like files on your computer. You need to erase the negative records and memories in order to make room for the positive. As you do this through the violet flame, you are freeing your soul to move on to higher levels of existence.

Psychotherapy gives you keys to understanding yourself and to making better choices in your life. You may gain resolution with someone you know because you've seen a negative record of the past and you've decided to make it positive in this life. When you add violet-flame decrees and service to those you have wronged, the combined action can clear the cause, effect, record and memory of these painful incidents.

And it's only by getting beyond those records, like Cynthia did, that you can clear the way for your soul to receive new opportunities. You can accelerate your soul's progress in this life and thus make your way more quickly to the goal of union with God.

Each time you balance the karma of a certain lifetime, your Higher Self may reveal to you the next past life that you need to tackle —and the next and the next. It's important not to feel burdened by the negative record of a past life. We have all made mistakes in the past or we wouldn't be here today. Forgive yourself and move on. Be grateful that you are here and that you have the opportunity to erase those records with the violet flame.

Once you start, keep on going. One step begins the trek of a thousand miles. Each time you transmute the records of a past life with the violet flame, you gain a new sense of your soul's liberation. And by and by you will realize that you are taking command of your soul's destiny.

9. **Expand the scope of your invocations to include cleaning up karmic debris in your house, your neighborhood and the planet.**

As you practice directing the violet flame to help others, you can begin to think of your aura as a violet-flame fountain where all whom you meet can come and drink. Remind yourself to always have that violet flame available for someone in need.

Not only does the violet flame dissolve your own karma, but it can also dissolve group or planetary karma that comes from such things as wars or accumulated injustices. In the next story you will see how Paula used the violet flame to transmute some of the most horrible records of the Civil War.

Paula knows that the violet flame can do more than transmute records of personal karma. It can also transmute the memories and karma of terrible events of the past, such as murders, injustices and even wars.

Paula and her family feel a strong connection with the South and the Civil War. One evening while she was in a group violet-flame decree session, she had a vision of the violet flame transmuting the records of one of the bloodiest battles of the Civil War—Shiloh.

The battle began early in the morning of April 6, 1862, when 42,000 Union soldiers were camping near Shiloh church, a simple log structure close to the Tennessee river. The troops, who expected no attack and did not dig defensive fortifications, were surprised by a Confederate army. The battle lasted two days and ended with the retreat of the Confederate army after 25,000 Union reinforcements arrived.

Yet it could hardly be called a Union victory. Over 20,000 Americans were killed—almost as many blue as gray. On the first night, the wounded left on the battlefield huddled together for warmth, with some dying in the arms of their enemies.

More Americans were killed during the battle of Shiloh than in any Civil War battle up to that time and more than in any of the three previous wars the nation had fought. One field was so covered with bodies that, as General Grant wrote, "it would have been possible to walk across [the entire field] in any direction, stepping on dead bodies without a foot touching the ground."[6]

Such a bloody battle left scars on the souls of everyone who participated—those who survived and those who perished. And it left a scar on the soul of a nation.

As Paula was decreeing, she had a vision of the violet flame transmuting the records of the event. She saw Shiloh at the end of the first day of fighting, when both sides had retreated, leaving the field to the dead and wounded. She wrote:

A light bleak rain was falling, causing the campfires to smoke, adding to the smoke from the day's fighting. This smoke hung low over a field terrible to behold. Dead, dying, wounded and exhausted men lay everywhere. I held my breath and beheld this scene and its pain.

Then, falling with the rain, came violet sparkles of light. This grew until the rain became a violet-flame downpour that eddied in pools around the bodies nearest to me. And then the real beauty began.

The violet light entered the hearts of the dead, who were all gray looking, and began to pulse out from there. From the deepest levels within their bodies, the violet light radiated out until the soldiers became violet, then pink and, finally, alive! Each soldier was surrounded by hundreds of angels and elemental beings who breathed the violet flame into him.

Wounded soldiers had the violet flame run over their wounds until they were sealed up and healed. As the soldiers were either healed or raised from the dead, they turned to help the heavenly beings bring others near them to life.

I saw one group of Confederate soldiers come alive and then help a Union drummer boy who had fallen in their midst. With great tenderness, they lifted him and his banner of the Union to their shoulders and paraded him around the field.

Thousands of men, bathed in the violet flame, just rolled out of death, stood up and hugged their fellowmen, regardless of uniform. I felt such infinite bliss as I watched this joyful vision spread across the entire battlefield thousands of lightbearers rejoicing, thoroughly removed from the pain of the past and in an awakened Union at last.

The vision expanded as if I was moving upward, so I could see for miles around the battlefield. Angels were bringing fathers, wives and family members who had suffered the loss of these brave men to this grand reunion.

From Shiloh, the violet flame swept over the other battlefields—Gettysburg, Chickamauga, Antietam. It went battlefield after battlefield and ever outward until I was looking down on North America and seeing the United States blazing like a violet jewel on the planet.

Paula was witnessing the transmutation of some of the records of these horrible battles. It's important for people to routinely direct the violet flame into these records for the healing of our planet. Even though the souls of those involved in this battle have most likely reincarnated, the record of the battle remains embedded in their psyches until it is transmuted by the violet flame.

Each time we direct the violet flame into records of battles and bloodshed, we transmute a little more of the karma and heal a little more of the scar. Paula's vision, then, demonstrated how each one of us can help to heal the scars of the world with the violet flame.

People have different experiences when they use violet-flame decrees. Some repeat them diligently for months before they have any confirmation that the decrees are working. Others get spectacular results the first time they open their mouths.

You can work out your own violet-flame routine in communion with your Higher Self. You can add the violet flame to your daily prayers or meditations, whatever they are.

If you haven't already skipped to the next section to try a violet-flame decree, I encourage you to try one now. Before you start, close your eyes and breathe a fervent prayer, asking your Higher Self to show you the value of violet flame in your life.

Repeat the decree 3 or 9 times to begin with. When you're ready, you can begin to increase your repetitions. Repeating a decree 36, 40, 108 or even 144 times can access more of God's power and your own spiritual resources.

I hope you will know the joy of becoming one of the thousands of people all over the world who have transformed their lives with this miracle solvent—the highest gift of God to the universe.

Decrees and visualizations

Decree:

TUBE OF LIGHT

Beloved I AM Presence bright,
Round me seal your tube of light
From Ascended Master flame
Called forth now in God's own name.
Let it keep my temple free
From all discord sent to me.

I AM calling forth violet fire
To blaze and transmute all desire,
Keeping on in Freedom's name
Till I AM one with the violet flame.

(Give three times)

Decree:

TRAVELING PROTECTION

You can give this decree in full voice when you are driving your car and say it softly on public transportation.

Lord Michael before, Lord Michael behind,
Lord Michael to the right, Lord Michael to
 the left,
Lord Michael above, Lord Michael below,
Lord Michael, Lord Michael wherever I go!

> I AM his love protecting here!
> I AM his love protecting here!
> I AM his love protecting here!

Decree:

GUARD, GUARD, GUARD US!

> Guard, guard, guard us!
> By the lightning of thy love!
> Guard, guard, guard us!
> By thy Great Self above!
> Guard, guard, guard us!
> By thy secret power of light!
> Guard, guard, guard us!
> By thy great and glorious might!
> And seal us safe forever
> In thy diamond heart of light!

Decree:

> I AM a Being of Violet Fire

This little decree can be the first violet-flame decree that you do and it can become a cornerstone of your violet-flame ritual.

Visualization:

As you say this decree, visualize the violet flame bathing and cleansing your aura. See the flames dissolve the debris in and around it. You are saying, "I AM the purity God desires!" because you want to purify your aura of everything that is not of God. When you give this decree, visualize any negative energy that contacts these flames being instantaneously transmuted into the light of God.

Decree:

> I AM a being of violet fire!
> I AM the purity God desires!

A variation of this decree is to insert the names of people you know or your hometown, nation or the planet. For example, you can say:

Earth is a planet of violet fire!
Earth is the purity God desires!

New York is a city of violet fire!
New York is the purity God desires!

MORE VIOLET FIRE

Visualization:

The decree "More Violet Fire" is known for its rhythm and for the spiraling action of the violet flame that follows the rhythm.

As you give this decree, commune with your I AM Presence. Feel the love of your "lovely God Presence" enfold you completely as you let go of all anger, worries, concerns and fears.

Visualize a waterfall of light descending

from your I AM Presence. See this light being released to you as streams of glistening
energy and then going forth to bless and
comfort those for whom you are praying.

See the violet flame dissolving the cause,
effect, record and memory of your own and
others' misdeeds. Don't forget to add your
own special images of what you want the
violet flame to accomplish. No problem is
too insignificant or too big to tackle with the
violet flame.

Decree:

> Lovely God Presence, I AM in me,
> Hear me now I do decree:
> Bring to pass each blessing for
>   which I call
> Upon the Holy Christ Self of each
>   and all!
>
> Let violet fire of Freedom roll
> Round the world to make all whole
> Saturate the earth and its people, too,

With increasing Christ-radiance
    shining through!

I AM this action from God above
Sustained by the hand of heaven's love,
Transmuting the causes of discord here,
Removing the cores so that none
    do fear.

I AM, I AM, I AM
The full power of Freedom's love
Raising all earth to heaven above
Violet fire now blazing bright
In living beauty is God's own light

Which right now and forever
Sets the world, myself, and all life
Eternally free in Ascended Master
    perfection!
Almighty I AM! Almighty I AM!
    Almighty I AM!

Decree:

Radiant Spiral Violet Flame

Radiant spiral violet flame,
　Descend, now blaze through me!
Radiant spiral violet flame,
　Set free, set free, set free!

Radiant violet flame, O come,
　Expand and blaze thy light through me!
Radiant violet flame, O come,
　Reveal God's power for all to see!
Radiant violet flame, O come,
　Awake the earth and set it free!

Radiance of the violet flame,
　Expand and blaze through me!
Radiance of the violet flame,
　Expand for all to see!
Radiance of the violet flame,
　Establish Mercy's outpost here!
Radiance of the violet flame,
　Come, transmute now all fear!

Decree:

VIOLET FLAME IS...

Breath of God inside each cell
I AM the violet flame
Pulsing out the cosmic time
I AM the violet flame
Energizing mind and heart
I AM the violet flame
Sustaining God's creation now
I AM the violet flame

With all love
With all love
With all love

Shimmering in a crystal cave
I AM the violet flame
Searching out all hidden pain
I AM the violet flame
Consuming cause and core of fear
I AM the violet flame
Revealing now the inner name
I AM the violet flame

With all peace
With all peace
With all peace

Flashing like a lightning bolt
I AM the violet flame
Stretching through the galaxies
I AM the violet flame
Connecting soul and Spirit now
I AM the violet flame
Raising you to cosmic heights
I AM the violet flame

With all power
With all power
With all power

NOTES

1. *The Voice of the I AM*, May 1936, p. 15.

2. *The Voice of the I AM*, January 1941, p. 20

3. Candace Pert, "The Chemical Communicators," in Bill Moyers, *Healing and the Mind* (New York: Doubleday, 1995), p. 189.

4. Andrew Weil, *Spontaneous Healing: How to Discover and Enhance Your Body's Natural Ability to Maintain and Heal Itself* (New York: Alfred A. Knopf, 1995), p. 85.

5. Michio Kaku, *Hyperspace: A Scientific Odyssey through Parallel Universes, Time Warps, and the Tenth Dimension* (New York: Anchor Books, Doubleday, 1994), p. 153.

6. Kenneth C. Davis, *Don't Know Much*

About the Civil War: Everything You Need to Know About America's Greatest Conflict but Never Learned (New York: William Morrow and Co., 1996), p. 227.

ADDITIONAL RESOURCES

If you would like to learn more about the spiritual techniques discussed in this book, we recommend beginning with *Spiritual Techniques to Heal Body, Mind and Soul,* 90-min. audiotape, listed here and advertised on the pages following.

AUDIOTAPES

Spiritual Techniques to Heal Body, Mind and Soul
by Elizabeth Clare Prophet
90 min.   devotional pace   #A99038 $10.95
(See ad on the following pages.)

Save the World with Violet Flame!
by Saint Germain
Tape 1   90 min.   devotional pace   #B88019 $7.95

Decrees and Songs by Mark L. Prophet
2-audiocassette album   3 hr.   devotional pace
#A8202 $14.95

BOOKS

Your Seven Energy Centers:
A Holistic Approach to Physical, Emotional and Spiritual Vitality by Elizabeth Clare Prophet
Softbound   4" x 6"   234 pages   #4485 $6.95

The Art of Practical Spirituality:
How to Bring More Passion, Creativity and Balance into Everyday Life by Elizabeth Clare Prophet
Softbound   4" x 6"   154 pages   #4484 $5.95

The Creative Power of Sound:
Affirmations to Create, Heal and Transform
by Elizabeth Clare Prophet
Softbound 4" x 6" 106 pages #4447 $5.95

The Lost Teachings of Jesus 4:
Finding the God Within
by Mark L. Prophet and Elizabeth Clare Prophet
Pocketbook 344 pages #2160 $6.99

Heart, Head and Hand Decrees
Booklet 48 pages #4444 $2.50

WALLET CARDS FOR VISUALIZATION

2¼" x 3½" full color $1.25 each
(with prayers and affirmations on the back)

Violet Fire #2944

Saint Germain #2947

Twin Flames #4450

Heart Chakra #4438

Secret Chamber of the Heart Chakra #4391

Archangel Michael #3571

Ascended Master Afra patron saint of Africa #4412

Chart of Your Divine Self 2⅛" x 3⅝" #1060

To place an order or request our free catalog, write
Summit University Press, PO Box 5000, Corwin Springs,
MT 59030-5000 USA or call 1-800-245-5445 or
406-848-9500. Fax 1-800-221-8307 or 406-848-9555.
Web site: www.summituniversitypress.com

SUMMIT UNIVERSITY  PRESS®

Summit University Press books are available from
fine bookstores everywhere. For a free catalog or
to place an order, please call 1-800-245-5445.

Spiritual Techniques to Heal Body, Mind and Soul

Elizabeth Clare Prophet, best-selling author and pioneer in practical spirituality, explores dynamic techniques for using the creative power of sound to transform our personal lives and bring spiritual solutions to today's global challenges.

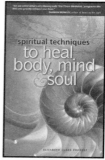

90-min. audiocassette
$10.95   A99038

SIDE 1: Learn how to combine visualizations, affirmations and meditation to access greater levels of your own inner potential. • Includes research from well-known experts on the science of mantra. • Shows how to access a high-frequency spiritual energy to improve relationships, increase mental clarity, and energize the body's seven energy centers.

SIDE 2: Join Elizabeth Clare Prophet as she puts these powerful techniques into practice. • Includes prayers, affirmations and decrees along with a nondenominational Rosary for World Peace. • Can be used daily to enhance your spiritual practice.

SUMMIT UNIVERSITY  PRESS®

To order call 1-800-245-5445

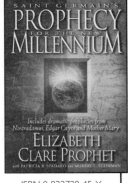

ELIZABETH CLARE PROPHET is a world-renowned author. Among her most popular books are *Your Seven Energy Centers: A Holistic Approach to Physical, Emotional and Spiritual Vitality* and others in her  Pocket Guides to Practical Spirituality series. Her breakthrough best-sellers include *Saint Germain's Prophecy for the New Millennium, The Lost Years of Jesus: Documentary Evidence of Jesus' 17-Year Journey to the East,* and *Reincarnation: The Missing Link in Christianity.*

Elizabeth Clare Prophet has pioneered techniques in practical spirituality, including the creative power of sound for personal growth and world transformation.